How to Learn a Foreign Language in Four Months

By Nicole Penn

Table of Contents:

Chapter 1 – Get Started Now and Don't Stop --3
Chapter 2 – Find Your Reason for Learning --12
Chapter 3 – How to Find the Time to Study --17
Chapter 4 – Learn the Sound of the Language --20
Chapter 5 – Building Vocabulary --29
Chapter 6 – Speaking --36
Chapter 7 – Reading --48
Chapter 8 – Writing --52
Chapter 9 – Dictionaries --55
Chapter 10 – Learn with Childlike Wonder, but Learn like an Adult --57

Chapter One – Get Started Now and Don't Stop

Many people are under the impression that mastering a foreign language requires formal study in a four-year university program or living abroad since childhood. The truth is there's more than one way to acquire a foreign language, and it doesn't always have to be a slow and lengthy process. If you cannot afford the luxury of taking a four-year university program to study a foreign language, you can choose to study the language on your own—at your own pace and possibly at a much faster speed.

Is it possible to learn a foreign language in four months instead of four years? The answer is yes. You can grasp the basics of a foreign language in a matter of months and set yourself on the right track toward fluency and mastery. However, I want to make it clear that there are no shortcuts when it comes to mastering a foreign language. Learning a foreign language in four months is made possible through a set of methods that can help you maximize your use of time for more effective and speedy learning. Nothing can substitute honest, hard work, especially when it comes to foreign language acquisition.

How can you cram four years of learning into four months and accomplish the impossible? First, you need to be ambitious and develop the right mindset before you start. Believe in yourself. Believe in your untapped potential. We're all equipped with the ability to perceive and comprehend language, as evidenced by the fact that you can speak your native language. Trust that you can make this impossible dream come true with your absolute, total commitment. Nothing is impossible to a willing heart and a determined mind.

The secret to learning a foreign language in four months is to get started right now and not stop. As the Chinese saying goes, "A journey of a thousand miles begins with a single step." Getting started is of paramount importance. It's the first step toward fluency. Overcome procrastination and hesitation, and resolve to embark on a journey of language, learning, and discovery.

Once you've decided that you would like to learn a new language, make it your top priority and give it your laser focus. This means you shouldn't try accomplishing two major missions at the same time. For instance, don't try to conquer Spanish in four months and prepare for your important bar exams at the same time. You will only spread yourself too thin this way. You will conquer a new language much faster if you can give it your undivided attention and devotion.

Also, don't waste too much energy searching for the perfect method or course to learn a new language. If you can stick to a routine religiously and put in the time and effort, even the most inefficient method can get you somewhere. "Just do it!" is a powerful attitude that can propel you forward.

I once stepped into a fast-food restaurant where the waiter told me that she would bring my meal to me within eighty seconds. She started a timer before she went about getting my meal. I thought to myself, "Why does she waste time telling me I can get my meal in eighty seconds? Why can't she just go get my meal directly? That will save her a few seconds!" It was a gimmick the restaurant used to impress the customers, but it didn't work so well, and the restaurant stopped doing that after a while. If you want to do something, just do it! Get started right away!

It's ok to read about other people's learning experiences and methods, but don't waste too much time searching for the perfect solution. That is why this is going to be a concise book on some key methods that I would like to share with you. Hopefully, they will be of some help to you.

To maximize efficiency in learning a new language, I recommend you make intense, concentrated, and uninterrupted efforts to familiarize yourself with the new language, preferably for at least four months. If you study intensely for two weeks and then stop for three months, chances are when you try to pick up from where you left off, you will have to go back to square one. I know this from my own painful and unsuccessful experience of learning French. I have tried to master the French language several times. Unfortunately, I stopped after I finished learning book one; another time, I stopped after learning book two. After that, two to three years went by before I decided to pick up learning French again for the third time. The rekindled interest was normally spurred by New Year's resolutions or other whims of my mind. Whenever I tried to pick up where I had left off, I had to start all over again, from lesson one of book one, to jog my memory of what I had learned. As of yet, I have not had any success with French using this on-and-off learning method.

Einstein once famously said that insanity is doing the same thing over and over and expecting different results. So I changed my learning strategy when I decided to learn Spanish. I achieved conversational fluency with extremely intensive and uninterrupted efforts after a little more than three months. Some may take three to four months to achieve conversational fluency; others may take longer than six months, it all depends on how many minutes you can commit to intensive studying. But the key is to get started and never give up midcourse.

Let's say it takes two weeks for you to finish learning book one. Two weeks of exposure to a foreign language is not enough time to forge any long-term memory of the new language. It's similar to losing weight—if you exercise strenuously for three days and then rest for one or two weeks, you will never be able to shed the extra fat from your body. Exercising for 45 minutes every day, consistently, is more effective than exercising intensely for a few days and then slacking off for one or two weeks. In the same way, learning a foreign language on and off will get you nowhere near fluency. If you can commit to learning a foreign language for four months, about 120 days, learning the language will become a part of your daily routine and you won't want to stop. Some say it takes 21 days to form a new habit, so 120 days is definitely enough time to help form the learning of a new language into a habit. After 120 days of continuous efforts, learning the language of your choice will become as natural as breathing.

Pick any foreign language. The textbooks for beginners usually consist of at least four textbooks, which can cover most grammar rules, tenses, conjugations, and high-frequency words. Once you have finished learning the first four textbooks, you're more likely to stick to learning that language than when you're stuck at the book one level.

If you have all the time in the world and study full-time, you can probably finish learning four textbooks in one month. If you have a full-time job or other obligations, such as taking care of a newborn baby, studying for fifteen hours per day is obviously out of the question. Your progress will be slower, but I still believe it's achievable to finish learning one textbook per month by making full use of every spare moment. You can definitely find the time to study if you make up your mind to do so. If you can manage one textbook per month, it will take you about four months to finish four textbooks. By that time, you will have become an advanced learner and reached a point where you won't want to give up.

Being a beginner is painful and sometimes discouraging, but once you tough it out through the first four textbooks, learning will become easier and feel more rewarding. Resolve to make unrelenting efforts to finish learning the first four books, no matter what. But be sure to choose up-to-date textbooks. Although textbooks published fifty years ago surely have their own merits, it's essential to keep abreast with the times.

When learning Spanish, I used a set of four textbooks: Aula 1, Aula 2, Aula 3, and Aula 4. These conversation-driven textbooks are richly illustrated and offer ample information about the history, geography, pop culture, and modern society of the Spanish-speaking world. Richly illustrated textbooks are interesting to look at, and the images make things more memorable. What's more important is that each lesson offers a summary of important structures and phrases you can use. There are also drills for you to practice what you have learned.

Go to a brick-and-mortar bookstore, browse through the textbooks on the shelf, and pick a few that look modern and appealing to you. After all, you have to spend a lot of time working on the textbooks. It's best if you select a textbook that is engaging.

All things are difficult before they get easy. Once you hit the magical book four, you will have gained a basic understanding of the language, which will give you more confidence and the impetus to learn more. The more you understand, the more you will like to know, and the easier it will get.

How do you make sure your love affair with a foreign language is not on and off? How do you make sure that you won't lose all the passion and steam?

You must commit to learning the language every single day, even if just for fifteen minutes a day. And don't you ever stop because once you stop, you'll lose your momentum and motivation. Discipline plays a critical role while learning a foreign language on your own. Exerting self-discipline can be a painful process, in which you keep fighting your inertia, procrastination, and various excuses to quit. Any worthy goal is worth the struggle! So, discipline yourself with a clear goal in mind, and you will be glad you did! You will be able to look back at your pain with pleasure in just four months.

To keep yourself on track, you can keep a journal of your learning progress starting from day one. You can upload your journal entry to your online blog, Facebook, or Twitter; or you can write in a small notepad, or start a note in the Evernote App or your cellphone's notebook. Record what you have learned and how much time you spent learning every day.

For example:

Day 1: Finished learning Lesson 1-Lesson 3.
Repeated after audio for thirty minutes.
Watched a 25-minute TV episode.

Day 2: Finished learning Lesson 4-Lesson 8.
Reviewed Lesson 1-Lesson 3.
Repeated after audio for forty minutes.
Watched a 25-minute TV episode.

Day 3: Too busy, didn't learn new lessons today.
Listened to the audio of old lessons while commuting to work.
...
Day 120 (after roughly four months): Finished reading ten news articles.
Finished reading one chapter of a book.
Listened to two chapters of an audiobook.
Watched a movie.
….

You get the idea. Keeping a journal helps prevent you from giving up halfway. It enables you to keep track of your progress and keep yourself encouraged and disciplined. It's like clocking in and showing up to study every day. If you miss a single day, be honest and write in the journal that you have not spent any time studying on that day. Resolve to pick it up the next day. Keeping such a journal will help you from quitting midcourse. Your persistence will finally pay off.

If you keep at it every single day, however small of an amount of time you can squeeze out for studying, the progress you make will surprise you. After four months of intensive studying, you will have moved up to a much higher level where you will have fewer reasons to give up because you are getting closer to the finish line. If you don't stay the course, all of your previous hard work will be in vain. Keep urging yourself to forge ahead on your journey to conquer a new language. When the views get better on the road, when you can use the language more aptly, you simply won't want to stop. A four-month passionate love affair may mellow into a lifelong companionship, in which you are inseparable from the language you have worked so hard to acquire.

Chapter Two – Find Your Reason for Learning

Learning a foreign language can be an arduous process: boring grammar drills, complex conjugations, and tenses, endless lists of new words.

To ensure you stay motivated, you need to find your reason for learning a foreign language. You are more likely to stay the course when you have a specific goal in mind. Some people learn a foreign language so that they can become more employable in the job market. Some people learn a foreign language just for the love of it. Others learn a foreign language because they have to immigrate to a new country or because they want to be a globetrotter. Whatever your reason for learning a new language, you need to be well aware of it and set a goal and time frame for yourself. If you don't have a strong reason to learn a foreign language, you probably won't go too far on your journey to conquer the language.

To find a good reason to learn, you can start by looking at the benefits of knowing a foreign language.

Fluency in a foreign language will open up doors of limitless opportunities for you. You will become a more valuable employee in an increasingly globalized world for a wide range of industries. If you speak a widely used language, traveling the world becomes easier and much more enjoyable. You will have access to firsthand information from a different language and do not have to rely on a translator.

Besides, some studies have shown that being bilingual or multilingual can delay the onset of Alzheimer's disease. While it's hard to verify the truth of such studies, learning a foreign language can actively engage your mind and help you develop your brain' s cognitive reserve, mental focus, and discipline. Learning new things constantly keeps your brain nimble.

To be able to speak a foreign language is to possess a different vision of the world. By learning Spanish, a language spoken in more than twenty countries, I have glimpsed into the culture and history of these twenty plus countries. It almost feels as if my vision of the world had been enlarged twentyfold because I wouldn't have known anything about these countries had I not learned Spanish. These countries and cultures would have been strangers who never crossed paths with me.

The ability to speak a foreign language gives you a new identity. Once you achieve fluency in a new language, speaking the language will become second nature; it will become a part of who you are. Isn't it cool to have another lifelong skill that no one can take away from you? You need to find your reason and your inner voice to enable yourself to stay the course.

Remind yourself regularly of your reason for learning. It might be helpful for you if you write down your reason and goal. A "reason and goal" statement can be written as follows:

"I want to be fluent in French so that I can get a promotion. I must finish learning four textbooks in four months..."

“I want to pass the TOEFL (Test of English as a Foreign Language) and GRE (Graduate Record Examinations) exams so that I can apply to study in a post-graduate program in the U.S. I will take the exams in three months."

“I want to be able to speak some Spanish so that I can travel to South America without too much difficulty. I will visit Mexico in December."

Having a well-defined reason and goal helps you discipline yourself and stay highly motivated.

I once came across a taxi driver who listened to Japanese tapes while driving. Curious about his motive for learning, I struck up a conversation with him. He told me he had fallen in love with a Japanese girl and that he was going to move to Japan with her. What can be a stronger motivator than love?

If you have a compelling reason to learn a foreign language, whatever it may be, you will find the time and discipline to do it, and you will learn faster than you would if you didn't have a specific goal in mind. Whether your motive is financial or emotional, it will definitely make you a more eager learner. So find your reason for learning and stay the course no matter what.

If you can develop a passion for the language, it will make a tremendous difference in your learning progress. Passion is the key ingredient that makes learning more enjoyable, more fun, and more rewarding. With passion, you can learn faster than people who just go through the motions.

If a child, who doesn't love music, is made to practice playing the piano a few hours per day, he will only practice grudgingly. If another child cannot live without music and often practices for hours out of his own will, which child stands a better chance of becoming the next musical prodigy? If you are genuinely passionate about something, you will be more willing to put in the hard work and go the extra mile to become better than your peers.

Students who enjoy learning languages will do more than what's expected of them to learn more than the curriculum, while students who show little interest in the language will do enough to pass an exam. It's passion that makes the difference between mediocrity and greatness.

How do you develop a passion for a language? For starters, you should pick a language whose culture you have an interest in. Learn about the history, geography, literature, must-see destinations, and celebrities of the country. Learn to appreciate the inherent beauty and musicality of the language by listening to songs and watching TV and movies in that language. Also, try to find opportunities to practice with native speakers of the language. The first time I conversed with a Spanish speaker, it felt as if I had discovered a new continent. I was euphoric about being able to utter coherent sentences and make myself understood in a foreign language. This immense feeling of satisfaction urged me to learn more. The more you know and open your heart to the new language, the less you will resent learning it.

If you can develop a genuine passion for the language itself, you will keep learning even when there are no immediate benefits in sight. All of the side benefits and perks of knowing a language will come naturally when you achieve fluency or even mastery.

If you become truly passionate about a language, you will find learning less boring. However, if you do feel bored browsing through vocabulary lists, you can change what you do. Your mind needs to rest after some intense efforts. Alternate between serious textbook learning and light-hearted activities such as watching TV or movies, listening to songs, reading jokes, doing word puzzles, or browsing through children's books and magazines in the new language. If you keep doing the same activity for a long time, boredom may creep in. Variety is the spice of life. Do something different every now and then so that your learning does not begin to get monotonous. That's how you keep the passion alive. You learn best when you are interested and happy.

Chapter Three – How to Find the Time to Study

If you have big chunks of uninterrupted time for studying, that's ideal. But if you have to juggle work and study or have to take care of attention-grabbing kids, you have to learn to make full use of the bits of spare time you have here and there to study. When you dedicate yourself to learning a new language, every spare moment should be utilized.

For instance, I have to commute for about two hours by metro to get to work and go home every day. I can do a lot while riding the metro: listen to an audiobook, learn a new lesson, read the latest news or even a few pages from a book. I highly recommend Bose noise-canceling earphones, which will be able to shield most of the background noise on public transport, thus maximizing your use of time. If you drive to work, you can listen to different audio materials while you drive.

I also listen to foreign language audiobooks while exercising and doing house chores like mopping, cooking, and washing dishes. Sometimes I use earphones if there's someone else in the house. When I am home alone, I connect my iPhone to a Bluetooth speaker. If you want to maximize your use of time, you can even listen to audio while taking a shower. You just need a small portable Bluetooth speaker that can amplify the sound. Most people spend at least fifteen minutes taking a shower, and this short period of time can be used to listen to the lesson you have just learned. Just put the audio on repeat, and after listening to the same audio piece four to five times, the unfamiliar sounds and words will start to take root in your mind.

You can also take out your vocabulary flash cards while waiting for a friend or a bus. Small bits of time can really add up. By making full use of any free time you can squeeze out of your day, surprisingly, you may be able to study for at least two to three hours. You just have to keep your goal in mind and avoid drifting into a mindless waste of time. Indeed, many of us waste too much time watching TV or funny YouTube videos, browsing Facebook, Twitter, Instagram, or simply chatting online. It's a great shame to squander so much time when we can use it more productively for language learning. If you want to, you can always find fifteen minutes to learn a few new words. So find the time or make the time to study, no excuses!

I once worked with an Indian accountant who used his left hand to work on a calculator and his right hand to write simultaneously. He told me that he trained himself to use both hands simultaneously, otherwise, he would not have enough time to finish his CPA accounting exams. He said it took a lot of practice to be able to do that. One hand to use the calculator, the other hand to write at the same time, all that just to have a little extra time to finish the exams!

Needless to say, I was tremendously impressed by his efforts to become a pro. High achievers are generally determined to put in the time and effort necessary to be successful. It takes focused determination and constant practice to become really good at something.

In the American movie The Pursuit of Happyness, Chris Garden didn't put down the phone while he made cold-calls to a list of potential clients so that he could gain nine minutes to make more calls and finish earlier. He also didn't drink water so that he wouldn't need to waste time going to the bathroom.

If you still complain about having no time to learn a foreign language, think about the example of using both hands simultaneously just to save a little time; think about Chris Garden making cold-calls nonstop with a parched throat. I am sure you can find the time to learn a few new words and a lesson or two.

There are many ways you can squeeze out some free time to study. It's really just a matter of whether you are willing to make the time or not. We are given the same amount of time every day. No one is getting more time than you. We all have 1,440 minutes or 86,400 seconds in a day and it's up to us to decide what to do with them. By using your time more effectively, you can accomplish far more than the next person. It's the minutes you put in that make all the difference.

Chapter Four – Learn the Sound of the Language

When we are babies we listen to our parents to learn our mother tongue. We learn to speak it before we can read it. Learning a foreign language as a teenager or an adult is a little bit different—we can learn to read and speak at the same time. Like learning our mother tongue, we can't really learn to speak if we don't listen to the sound of the language. As a beginner, I recommend you choose only textbooks that come with audio. You can keep silent articles and books for when you become an advanced learner.

The beginning is always excruciatingly hard because you have to familiarize yourself with unfamiliar sounds and new ways of speaking. Fortunately, repetition can help you forge an almost indelible memory. I recommend listening to the audio of a new text at least five to ten times when you first learn the lesson. Repeating the process ten times is not a be-all-end-all effort. Chances are you will only retain fifty percent of the information the first time you learn a lesson. There's no need to repeat too many times in one go, as repetition will become too mechanical and mind numbing after a while. Instead, choose to review the lesson at another time. Listen to the old lessons a few more times in the coming week before learning the next lesson. After reviewing the lesson two to three times, you may be able to retain about eighty percent of the information. Reviewing the lessons you have learned is critical for forging long-term memory. You can listen to the audio of old lessons while driving, exercising, taking a walk, or doing house chores, which makes reviewing lessons effortless.

However, I'd like to point out that you don't have wait until you can retain 100 percent of the information before you start a new lesson. Just keep moving forward and learning new lessons, which are often built on the basis of older lessons. In this sense, learning new lessons can reinforce what you have already learned.

If you keep reviewing the same lesson, you will feel that you are not making progress and become discouraged. If you can understand eighty percent of a lesson, that's already quite good. It's ok to move on to the next lesson. You can always come back to review the old lesson. Moving on to the next lesson will give you a sense of accomplishment and more impetus to forge ahead. As you learn more lessons, what you didn't quite understand in the beginning becomes clearer. Words start to stick in your mind because of repeated exposure.

After you finish learning four textbooks, you can upgrade to news with audio, short stories and articles with audio, and short audiobooks with transcripts. For starters, you can listen to short news stories that typically last three to five minutes. You can play the news piece on repeat until you feel you have learned the pronunciation and meaning of each word. Such short audio pieces are easily digestible, which makes learning pleasant and rewarding.

Also, look for apps that deliver daily news with audio. The news is a great vessel to learn about a wide variety of topics in a foreign language. To be fluent, you have to be able to talk about things beyond the weather and foods.

www.audible.com has a wide variety of ...n different languages, but those ...s typically last seven to ten hours and ...ally do not come with transcripts. I do not recommend audiobooks without scripts for beginners. You can save Audible audiobooks for immersion for when you are a much more advanced learner. Further, www.librivox.org offers free public domain audiobooks in 36 languages. You can also download the Librivox app from the iPhone App Store. The Gutenberg Project (www.gutenberg.org) offers more than 50,000 free e-books and some audiobooks as well. If you want to learn French, you can check out www.litteratureaudio.com, which offers more than 5,000 free French literature e-books and audiobooks.

There's a tremendous amount of free resources available on the Internet in this digital age. For example, if you happen to be learning one of the five official languages of the United Nations—Chinese, English, French, Russian and Spanish—you can visit the UN's website www.un.org for free resources such as speeches, the latest news, videos, and podcasts in these five languages. You can teach yourself a new language using these resources at minimal cost.

As a beginner, you can look for some short and sweet audiobooks with scripts in the iPhone App Store. I know for a fact there are many affordable short audiobooks with scripts in Spanish, French, and Japanese in the iPhone App Store. You will probably find audiobooks in other languages as well. Those audiobooks typically last for about half an hour. You can study the scripts first, learn new words, and then listen to the audiobooks at least a dozen times.

I bought dozens of Spanish audiobooks produced by Online Studio Productions from the iPhone App Store. These Spanish audiobooks are non-fiction books, mostly about biographies, country profiles, history, culture, geography, and celebrities. These audiobooks last about thirty minutes on average, and they're like a miniature textbook in and of itself; they're short and sweet, with lots of useful information. What's best about these audiobooks is that they all come with word-for-word transcripts, which enables me to study each word's pronunciation, spelling, and meaning conveniently.

In a four-month intensive learning program, I recommend saving such audiobooks for the fourth month. I can listen to at least one to six such audiobooks per day, depending on the free time at my disposal. After listening to these audiobooks, I find that I have greatly improved my listening comprehension of the Spanish language while expanding my vocabulary. The contents of these audiobooks are incredibly diverse compared to the textbooks I started with. As an added bonus, I have personally gained a much deeper understanding of the history and culture of Hispanic countries.

When learning a language, it's important to match audio with scripts. In the award-winning movie The Reader (2008), starring Kate Winslet and David Ross, a fifteen-year-old boy has an affair with a woman twice his age. The woman hides her illiteracy because of her embarrassment and thus has the boy read books to her. The woman later disappears for some years, and the boy later becomes a law student and is surprised to see her again in a court trial for war crimes. The woman is tried for her time as a prison guard at the Auschwitz concentration camp. Her fellow prison guards frame her for writing an incriminating report when she actually didn't know how to read and write. Ashamed of her own illiteracy, she admits to writing the report and declines to show her writing to the court to prove her innocence. As a result, she is sentenced to prison for life. Twenty years later, the boy has grown up to be a lawyer and thinks of reconnecting with her. He records stories for the woman and sends dozens of cassettes to her. The woman also checks out books from a prison library to match the audiotapes. She is then able to teach herself to read and write by matching the audio to the book word for word, sentence by sentence. By matching sound with scripts, you too can learn the pronunciation and spelling of words at the same time.

There's a French film called My Afternoons with Margueritte (2010) (French: La tête en friche). The film tells the story of a nearly illiterate man, Germain, who bonds with a 95-year-old woman Margueritte, who enjoys reading. Germain couldn't read very well, partly because he had a negligent mother and a teacher who belittled him in class when he was young. Germain encounters Margueritte in a park and starts to bond with her. Margueritte begins reading excerpts from her novel to Germain, who has an excellent aural memory. To help Germain learn to read, Margueritte gives him a dictionary as a present, but Germain becomes frustrated when he cannot find any words in the dictionary without first knowing the spelling of the word.

When learning a language—even your mother tongue—it's important to match audio and scripts so that you can learn to speak and write. Both movies, The Reader and My Afternoons with Margueritte, attest to this point.

I do not recommend using dictation to improve listening skills. If there are some words you don't know, no matter how many times you listen to the audio, you still won't know those words. Dictation is a very time-consuming and ineffective method. I recommend always matching audio with scripts. Listen to the audio while reading the scripts and look up every new word. As you expand your vocabulary and deepen your understanding of the language, you will reach a point where you won't need subtitles to understand movies, and you can then listen to audiobooks without scripts for immersion.

As a beginner in learning a foreign language, just consider yourself illiterate in the foreign language. You have to learn to speak and write from the beginning. Only by matching audio with scripts can you improve your listening comprehension, speaking, and writing abilities.

Once you get past the textbook learning or the beginner level, learning becomes easier and gives you a greater sense of accomplishment.

In addition to news and audiobooks, you can also watch TV series and movies in a foreign language. While audiobooks and news programs are excellent materials for learning a foreign language, people in real life do not talk like audiobook narrators and news broadcasters, who typically enunciate each word carefully and speak at a slower than normal speed. If you don't have the luxury to live in the country where the language is spoken, you can watch TV series and movies from that country to get used to how most of the people talk there. In this sense, watching TV and movies is a required course for learning a foreign language.

TV and movies are a great window into how real people talk and how a language is used in different settings. You don't have to wait until you can fully understand a TV sitcom to watch TV in a foreign language. You can start watching short TV series as soon as you grasp a basic vocabulary of the language. When you can understand bits of the TV conversations, you will feel encouraged and want to learn more. Of course, don't spend big chunks of time watching TV when you can only understand a little. Your priority should be learning more lessons and expanding your vocabulary in the beginning. You can reward yourself by watching a short TV sitcom when you are tired of working on the textbook.

Besides, by watching TV and movies, you can create an immersive environment for yourself. You don't have to go to a foreign country for immersion. Many Chinese people, who have lived in the U.S. for years, cannot speak English properly. Dually, many westerners who have worked in Hong Kong for years cannot speak much Cantonese. Thus, an immersive environment is only effective when you make conscious efforts to learn more about the language.

Listening to popular songs is another good way to familiarize yourself with the sound of a language and pick up a few new words and phrases while relaxing. If you can develop a keen interest in the language and the culture, you will study with a stronger motivation and sense of enjoyment.

One of my overriding passions is traveling the world and experiencing different cultures. I browsed photos of famous tourist attractions in Latin American countries to find more incentive to learn. I was deeply fascinated by Machu Picchu in Peru, the Uyuni Salt Flats in Bolivia, and Easter Island in Chile and vowed to travel to these breathtaking places one day. I also watched tourism videos about these countries and I found that the more I learned about these South American countries and Spain, the more I wanted to visit them and learn Spanish. I have developed a true passion for Spanish and Spanish-speaking countries.

I know a Chinese girl whose remote relatives were killed by Japanese invaders in the 1940s. Naturally, she harbored resentment against the Japanese due to this history. She later came across a Japanese song that completely enchanted her, although she couldn't understand a word of Japanese. Afterward, she learned more about the singer and was even more hooked. She managed to put her resentment and vendetta aside and decided to take up Japanese lessons because she wanted to understand what the singer was singing. After a few months of intensive learning, she became conversational in Japanese and traveled to Japan to attend the singer's concert in Japan. It was a dream come true for her, getting up close to a singer she so admired.

Like I said, you need to find your reason for learning a foreign language. Your motive can be emotional or financial. Whatever your motive, it can propel you to learn more, and faster at that.

Chapter Five - Building Vocabulary

Some people consider the process of learning new words a chore, while I relish the opportunity to learn new words and new things.

It's also a good opportunity to eliminate obstacles and further a better understanding. Having a positive mindset about building your vocabulary is critical for more effective learning. Instead of memorizing new words grudgingly, your eyes should twinkle with excitement at the sight of a new word, because it's an opportunity to eliminate one more enemy on your journey toward fluency and mastery.

Vocabulary and grammar rules are the fundamental building blocks for comprehension. Once you have grasped the most commonly used words and the basic grammatical rules, comprehension comes naturally.

Here's a rule of thumb for learning new words: do not memorize words only. Learn new words in a sentence so that you know how to use a word in context. This may seem more time-consuming than memorizing words only, but in the long run, learning words in sentences pays off. It's not enough to know the meaning of a word, it's important to know how to use the word to express an idea. This is also how you learn to form cohesive sentences and speak fluently.

As a beginner, it's useful to learn some sentences by heart as well, especially sentences you can use in your daily life.

Sentences such as "This is a chair" or "I want to kill you" are not socially functional sentences. Learn sentences that you can actually use to communicate with people under different circumstances.

Whenever I encounter a new word, I look it up in a big dictionary and copy the definition and sample sentences on a piece of paper to reinforce my understanding and memory of the new word and its uses. While you flip through a dictionary, you can also pick up other new words and phrases as well. On the surface, it's a very time-consuming process, but in reality, the process helps you gain a true understanding of how a new word can be used. With this kind of knowledge, you upgrade from being a mere beginner to a fluent language user.

Learning a new word is not just about learning its pronunciation, spelling, and meaning. Only when you know how to use the word in context, how to make a sentence using the new word, can you claim to truly know the word. If you have a large vocabulary, but you cannot speak or write, you are not hitting the mark just yet. Knowing how to use words to form cohesive speech is true comprehension.

It's imperative that you read the definition and sample sentences of a new word to gain a better understanding. While doing this may slow you down in the beginning, it will actually accelerate your learning in the long run because of the solid groundwork it helps you lay down.

There are two ways to build your vocabulary:

1. You can make concentrated efforts to learn new words from vocabulary-building books, preferably vocabulary lists that come with sample sentences and audio.

For example, to expand my Spanish vocabulary, I bought a Spanish vocabulary book by Barron's: Mastering Spanish Vocabulary with Audio Mp3: A Thematic Approach. This vocabulary book offers lists of words under different themes. The sample sentences and audio helped me learn about 6,000 Spanish words easily.

Studying vocabulary books is a little bit dry and boring, but it can help you increase your vocabulary dramatically. There are books on the most commonly used verbs, idioms, and assorted words for different topics. Intense, concentrated efforts can help you learn a great number of new words within a short time frame. Review the vocabulary books a few times for best results. I highly recommend studying vocabulary books with concentrated efforts if you want to learn a foreign language in four months. There are vocabulary books that come with pictures and visual aid, like audio, that can also facilitate learning and memory. Use both your visual and aural memory for better results.

Pick up a few picture dictionaries for children. Such dictionaries are often written in an easy-to-understand way. Pictures make vocabulary lists less dry and facilitate memory.

Consider yourself a child when learning a foreign language. It helps to start with easy and basic stuff and a childlike curiosity. After you finish reading a few children's picture dictionaries, you can pick up a copy of DK Visual Dictionary, which can help you develop a more advanced vocabulary about daily objects and different themes. There are DK Visual Dictionaries available in multiple languages.

Purchase a dictionary of synonyms and antonyms, preferably a dictionary with sample sentences. Forget about dictionaries that only give you dry lists of words or dictionaries that have tiny font because they are difficult and boring to read and it's easy to get frustrated and just give up. Choose a dictionary that has an eye-friendly font that's pleasant to read.

Pick up a few vocabulary books on high-frequency words, commonly used verbs, and phrases. Preferably books that come with sample sentences and audio. If you can master 3,000 to 4,000 high-frequency words, you may be able to cover ninety percent of daily conversational needs. Other words with lower frequency are just like icing on the cake, you can add the icing on later, but you need to make the cake first. Focus on the high-frequency, essential words of a language, and you will get off to a better start.

2. You can also learn new words while reading, which is more fun than studying vocabulary lists. This can be a continuous, more relaxed process compared with perusing vocabulary lists. Pick an article that has about ten to twenty new words and look up every new word in a dictionary. Make a habit of reading at least two to three short articles per day, and learn every new word in the articles. When you have an advanced command of the language, you can start reading full-length books for immersion. If you persist, your vocabulary will expand. This can be an ongoing way of learning, and it feels less painful than learning 100 new words a day using a vocabulary-building book. I recommend using both methods to acquire new words.

While you read to expand your vocabulary, it's wise to choose articles that have only about ten to twenty new words in them so that you don't get too discouraged by the challenge. If you don't know half of the words in an article, you may lose heart. Adopt a gradual and incremental method when it comes to building your vocabulary. Don't choose articles that have too many new words, for it will make learning look like an insurmountable barrier.

Another important principle of learning new words is not to do any guesswork. Never guess the meaning of a word unless you are taking an exam and cannot look it up in a dictionary. You don't need to win the speedy reading championship when you are building up your vocabulary. If you don't take the trouble to look up a new word, you may never learn to use it correctly.

As previously mentioned, whenever I encounter a new word, I look it up in a dictionary. I recommend you do the same. It may slow the reading process in the beginning, but as you accumulate your vocabulary you will not need to stop to check new words as often, and your reading speed will gradually pick up. The key is not how fast you can read; it is how much you can absorb and internalize.

If you find using the bulky paper dictionary troublesome, you can read articles and books on Kindle, which enables you to check the definition of a word by pressing the word with your finger.

If you have more time at your disposal, you can write down the definition and sample sentences on a piece of paper. When you copy those sentences, you are forced to pay close attention to the spelling, the collocation, and the sentence structure, which will help you understand and memorize the new word. If you are short of time, just give the definition a close look.

If you look up the words that you are struggling to remember, they will gradually make an impression and stick in your mind. You can write new words on Post-its and stick them to whatever you see fit. Surround yourself with Post-its or flash cards of the new words. Expose yourself repeatedly to the new words. Learning new words is like courting a girl. You need to create opportunities to see the girl more often so that you can make an impression and get close to her. Likewise, you need to see the new words more often so that you can develop a love affair with the new language.

Some words are easier to remember than others. Just don't get frustrated when you cannot recall the meaning of a word that looks familiar. What you need is to expose yourself to the word a few more times to forge your long-term memory. Even people with a good memory cannot memorize every single new word by reading it only once.

Long-term memory comes from comprehension and repeated exposure.

Chapter Six - Speaking

I emphasize using audio and scripts at the same time when you are a beginner because listening to audio enables you to learn the correct pronunciation of each word, which is the foundation of speaking. If you don't even know how a particular word is pronounced, you just cannot form speech.

Babies listen to their parents who repeat simple words hundreds of times before they can utter the same words. Consider yourself a baby while learning a foreign language. Listen keenly to the audio first, and then repeat after the audio a dozen times. Opening your mouth to imitate the audio is a critical first step toward speaking fluently. Start working on pronunciation from the very beginning to avoid speaking with a bad accent, which will make it difficult for people to understand you.

Talking requires you to move the muscles of your mouth. Listening to tapes alone cannot help you get used to speaking a new language. You have to open your mouth, move your muscles, and imitate the sound you hear. Watch the face of a native speaker and pay attention to his mouth movements while he speaks. Ask a native speaker to help you with words that are difficult to pronounce whenever you get a chance.

Shadowing is a simple technique you can use to learn to speak better in a foreign language.

Shadowing means you shadow the audio you are listening to, repeat after the audio word for word, and imitate the pronunciation, intonation, musicality, and rhythm of the audio, like a shadow. The more you shadow, the more fluently you will be able to speak, and the faster you will find your own voice in the foreign language.

Shadowing is a technique many interpreters use to train themselves to speak while listening. Aim to set aside at least half an hour for shadowing every day.

Learning to speak properly is no easy task. In the movie My Fair Lady (1964), a Cockney flower girl by the name of Eliza Doolittle took English speech lessons from a phonetic professor named Henry Higgins. She was made to practice until 3 a.m. Professor Higgins gave her a pep talk to keep her motivated, "Eliza, if I can go on with a blistering headache, you can. I know your headaches. I know you are tired. I know your nerves are as raw as meat in a butcher's window. But think what you are trying to accomplish. Just think what you're dealing with. The majesty and grandeur of the English language, it's the greatest possession we have. The noblest thoughts that ever flowed through the hearts of men are contained in its extraordinary, imaginative, and musical mixtures of sounds. And that's what you've set yourself out to conquer, Eliza. And conquer it, you will."

After a few months of intensive speech and etiquette training, Eliza was transformed into an upper-class lady, and she was even mistaken for a foreign princess at a ball. Whenever you think of quitting, think of what you set out to accomplish, think of your reason for learning. Like Eliza, you will be able to transform yourself with your persistent efforts.

Professor Higgins required Eliza to enunciate each word and be clear as a bell when she spoke. This requirement can apply to anyone who's learning to speak properly. To be fluent, the key is not to speak as fast as you can. Speaking fast is not equivalent to being fluent. To get the enunciation of each word correct, practice pronouncing each syllable so that people can understand you easily. And based on good enunciation and pronunciation, you can learn to speak faster to make your speech flow.

Getting the pronunciation of words right is the first step to speaking. How do you learn to actually speak in sentences? To get yourself going, you can memorize some useful phrases and sentences.

Functional sentences such as:
"I'd like to go to the airport."
"Can you give me a discount?"
"You are very kind."

Such sentences will come in handy when you interact with real people. Read the sentences out loud a few times until you can blurt them out effortlessly.

Even in book one, there are a lot of functional sentences. Learn to speak from book one, from day one. You don't have to wait until you become an intermediate or advanced learner to be able to speak. You also don't need to have a huge vocabulary to begin to speak.

When babies start to talk, they start with simple words. When they grow to be two to three years old, they can say simple sentences; although their enunciation is not always clear and their grammar not always correct, they still manage to communicate their thoughts with their very limited vocabulary. So, you don't really need to possess a huge vocabulary to be able to start talking. What you need to do is learn to use whatever words, phrases, and sentences you already know and learn to speak from book one, lesson one, and day one! At the book one level, you should at least be able to talk like a child in the new language.

One of the reasons being a beginner is so painful is because you feel you cannot communicate in the language. This is exactly why you should learn to speak from day one to give yourself some sense of progress and accomplishment. When you feel you're making progress, learning feels less painful and more rewarding.

In each lesson, there are some useful phrases and sentences. Memorize those sentences,
or try making some changes to the sentences to make them relevant to yourself.

For example, here are a few Spanish sentences from Lesson One of my Spanish textbook, Aula 1 (Book One):

"Me llamo Katia Vigny. Tengo 23 años." – My name is Katia Vigny. I am 23 years old.

You can change the name to your real name and the number to your real age and make a sentence that's relevant to yourself.

"Me llamo Michael Johnson. Tengo 28 años." - My name is Michael Johnson. I am 28 years old.

You see, it's not that difficult to speak from Day One. You can start with some simple sentences. Embrace your progress and keep encouraging yourself to learn more sentences to describe yourself and things that are relevant to you. By making the sentences relevant to you, it will be easier for you to remember them - and those sentences will come in handy someday.

Here's another paragraph from Lesson 3 of Aula 1:

"China es un país muy grande y muy interesante. Esta en Asia y la capital es Pequín. Es el país más poblado del mundo. La lengua oficial es el chino, pero hay muchos dialectos y otras lenguas."

(China is a very big and interesting country. It's in Asia and its capital is Beijing. It's the most populous country in the world. The official language is Chinese, but there are many dialects and other languages.)

You can first memorize the whole paragraph to learn new words, phrases, and structures. Then you can change the subjects, objects, adjectives, and adverbs in the paragraph to make your own sentences. Let me show you how.

"China es un país muy grande y muy interesante." - China is a very big and interesting country.

You can change the subject from "China" to "the United States" - Los Estados Unidos es un país muy grande y muy interesante. (The United States is a very big and interesting country.)

"Está en Asia y la capital es Pequín." - You can change "Asia" to "América" and replace "Pequín" with "Washington D.C. - "Está en América y la capital es Washington D.C."

"Es el país más poblado del mundo." - It's the most populous country in the world.
You can change "poblado"(populous) into "rico" (rich) - "Es el país más rico del mundo." - It's the richest country in the world.

"La lengua oficial es el chino". - The official language is Chinese.
You can change "chino" into "inglés" (English) - "La lengua oficial es inglés"

By changing a few words, you can describe China and the United States in Spanish. You see, at Lesson 3 of Book One level, you can write a short paragraph to describe the United States!

If you know 5 nouns, 5 verbs, and 5 adjectives, you may be able to create 125 sentences. This is how you learn to speak and write in a foreign language quickly. I used this method to quickly learn many useful Spanish sentences and I achieved conversational fluency within a matter of months because my learning method is sentence-based.

Memorize useful sentences from each lesson. I like to compare learning a new lesson to fishing: the sentences you master are the fish you get at the end of the day. At the end of a fishing day, you count how many fish you have caught. At the end of each lesson, you should also count how many sentences you have learned; how many sentences you can speak. Don't count the words; count the sentences. If you want to be able to speak sooner rather than later, memorize the sentences, make your own sentences, and never memorize words in isolation without a sentence context.

In addition to a set of textbooks, you can get a phrasebook and learn to speak some simple phrases right from the beginning. You don't have to fully understand the grammar rules in the beginning; simply memorize the sentences and learn to use them in your speech. As you progress with your study, those grammar rules will become clearer to you.

Do not be shy about practicing with real people. When I was just beginning to learn Spanish, my friend took me to a Mexican restaurant. I started talking to a Mexican waiter in Spanish, "Tengo hambre." (I'm hungry.) It was hilarious. Actually, it's a useful sentence to know. It tells people that you need food, not water. That's what I could remember and blurt out at that moment. And I continued to order from the menu with my broken Spanish. Actually using the language will make you feel that you are getting somewhere with the language, and that you have a sense of accomplishment, however small it may be.

Do not worry about making mistakes when you speak, because you won't be judged harshly as a beginner. If you worry about being perfect, you will become verbally paralyzed. Most people will be incredibly encouraging and patient when they see a foreigner trying to speak their language. So, losing face should be the least of your concern. Babies cannot enunciate every word very well when they start to speak, but their speech improves as they grow up. Your foreign language proficiency will also grow as you advance on your journey.

You can also pick up some colloquial dictionaries and books on conversations. There are many books available, such as 900 Sentences in French/Spanish. Memorizing sentences for daily conversations can be a good start toward speaking fluently.

Once you have developed an advanced vocabulary, I recommend watching short TV series and movies with word-for-word subtitles. Personally, I prefer short TV sitcoms over 2-hour movies. Pick a few TV episodes that run about 25-40 minutes, and watch each episode at least a few times. Look up each new word in the dictionary so that you are actually learning something new.

Do not just settle for only roughly understanding the plot. Be an active listener. Pay attention to how people talk, how an idea is expressed and how words are pronounced and linked together. Repeat after the actors and actresses. In doing so, you can improve your pronunciation, intonation, and cadence. This will definitely help you remember some useful sentences.

Watching a video only once is not like "water off a duck's back". Instead, you may just end up only having a fuzzy idea of the plot. In-depth learning generates greater benefits, which is why it is a good idea to watch each video at least a couple of times. Repetition makes learning and comprehension easier. Choose short TV sitcoms and videos that interest you. If you find the video compelling, you likely won't mind watching these clips more than once.

This book is written for people around the world who want to learn a foreign language. The methods I talk about can be applied to learning any language under the sun. If you are from a non-English-speaking country and want to learn English, I highly recommend TED speeches (www.ted.com). TED speeches typically last about 10-20 minutes and often come with subtitles in a few languages. You can choose the English subtitles option and download the TED videos to your computer so that you can watch them even when you don't have access to the Internet. You can even upload some TED videos to your cell phone or tablet so that you can watch them while you are on the go. There are more than 2000 TED talks on a wide variety of topics. Even for native speakers of English, TED talks can be an exceptional source of intellectual and spiritual inspiration. Watching all the TED talks will definitely help you expand your horizons and be closer to mastering the English vocabulary. Always turn on the subtitles when you watch a TED so that you can study each spoken word. Watch at least one or two TED talks per day. Repeat after the speaker to learn the pronunciation and the rhythm of the speech. Gradually, your tongue will feel agiler and you will feel more comfortable speaking the foreign language. Shadowing the speaker will help you to learn to speak as fluently as a native speaker.

If you are learning languages other than English, look for video programs similar to TED talks. These include short and sweet interviews, speeches by politicians and luminaries and short sit-coms (preferably with subtitles). If you have access to only a few DVDs, CDs, and tapes, listen to those materials over and over again. If you are more resourceful, extensive exposure to different video and audio materials will be very helpful for developing a better command of the language.

When speaking and writing in a foreign language, do not translate from your mother tongue. Instead, reflect on what you have learned about the foreign language in order to try to speak and write like a native speaker. What if you think of a fancy sentence in your mother tongue, but you don't know how to express it in a foreign language? My advice is to give up the fancy idea conceived in your mother tongue. Only speak what you know in the foreign language.

It doesn't matter if you can only express your ideas with simple words in the foreign language, as long as it is how a native speaker talks. It's better than translating from your mother tongue and risk sounding incorrect and outlandish. Do not struggle between your mother tongue and the foreign language. Pay attention to how the native speakers talk, imitate them, copy their sentence structures and expressions. You don't have to reinvent the language, just learn how the language is used. You may start with some rote memory of sentences, but once you gain a better understanding of the language, you will be able to make your own sentences.

Whatever materials you are using, summarize and memorize useful sentences from the materials. Break down articles and paragraphs into useful sentences.

Read a sentence a few times, and then recall each sentence word-for-word without looking at the sentence. Check whether you can recall the sentence correctly. If not, read the sentence again and try recalling the sentence again until you get it right. This is a simple yet useful memorization exercise that can help you learn to speak and write like a native speaker.

When I learned Spanish, I noted down some sentences I liked on some small flash cards and took out the flash cards to read those sentences out loud whenever I had a few minutes. Repeated exposure solidified my memory and understanding of those sentences, and I was able to actually use some of the sentences in my conversations with Spanish-speaking people.

When you read, try changing the subject of a sentence to "I" so you can imagine yourself speaking under different scenarios. By doing this, you will become more emotionally engaged with learning. Let me show you how to do it.

Here's a short paragraph from my Spanish textbook:
"Ema es la madre de Luis. Es enfermera. Trabaja en un hospital pequeño."
(Ema is the mother of Luis. She's a nurse. She works in a small hospital.)

Vocabulary:
Madre - mother
Enfermera - female nurse

Trabaja – she works
Trabajo – I work
Pequeño – small
Soy – I am

I can change the subject from Ema to "I": "Soy la madre de Luis. Soy enfermera. Trabajo en un hospital pequeño. (I am Luis' mother. I am a nurse. I work in a small hospital.)

By changing the subject, you make the sentence more relevant to yourself, and you also get to practice verb conjugations.

Another trick to help you speak better is to find a study partner, language exchange partner or a tutor. Practice with your partner or tutor. If you cannot afford to pay a tutor for private lessons, you can post an ad on an online forum such as on Craiglist and tell people about your interest in finding a language exchange partner. If you are learning Spanish, and your mother tongue is English, you can offer to teach a Spanish-speaking person English if that person happens to be learning English. Chances are you will get a few replies to your post. You may also attract someone who may offer you free lessons.

A Chinese friend of mine went to study in Germany, so she posted an ad on the university bulletin board seeking a language practice partner. A retired German old lady saw her ad and offered to teach her German for free. Many retired old people are often lonely and want to be more socially engaged by talking to people. Some may agree to teach you for very little money or even free of charge. It's a win-win for both.

Chapter Seven - Reading

People learn a foreign language with different goals and expectations. Some want to be fluent on all fronts, others just want to develop reading competency so that they can read contracts, technical literature or emails. Whatever your goal for reading proficiency, adopt a step-by-step approach to enhance your reading comprehension.

When choosing reading materials, it's important not to choose articles or books that have too many words you don't know. If you cannot understand 50% of the words in an article, you will soon become disheartened by the barriers that pop up every now and then. Worst scenario, you may even give up in frustration. To make your life easier, you can save such articles for later when you have a larger vocabulary. For now, choose articles that are suited to your current level. I recommend choosing articles that have about 10-20 new words so that you can learn something new and minimize the risk of feeling discouraged.

When you feel comfortable reading news articles, you can subscribe to some magazines and newspapers. If you subscribe to a daily newspaper, accept the fact that it's impossible to read all articles in the newspaper. Just make a habit of reading at least 3-5 news articles a day, and you will make incremental progress on many fronts. A newspaper covers many facets of the language and culture. It's a great gateway to have a glimpse into the country behind the language.

As for full-length books, I recommend focusing on non-fiction books in the beginning. The wording, style and sentence structures in non-fiction books are more direct, and a lot of the sentences from non-fiction books can be used in speaking as well. By contrast, novels tend to have more complex sentence structures that are harder to understand. You can start with relatively simpler non-fiction books that discuss self-improvement and management. As your knowledge builds, you can then move on to books with more specialized areas.

Avoid novels from a few centuries ago as the language may be a bit outdated or even archaic. Alternatively, you can read rewritten, simplified modern versions of classic novels, preferably with audio. Such simplified versions of classics are generally created for children and foreigners who learn the language as a second language. Each country has its own classic literature that has found its way into its values, proverbs, and culture. So it helps to read some of the famous classic novels from that country.

If you enjoy reading literature, you can also choose novels written by contemporary writers so that you can learn authentic and contemporary ways of speaking and writing. You wouldn't want to sound like someone from the eighteenth century. Save the classics for later as they only make things more complicated than necessary for beginners.

To make reading easier, consider purchasing an e-book reader such as the Amazon Kindle, which is by far one of the best inventions of the twenty-first century. Amazon Kindle devices, though small, can hold hundreds of e-books, eliminating the need to lug heavy books around. You can go a step further and also install a few dictionaries on your Kindle; learning new words will no longer be a pain in the neck. The Kindle enables you to look up the meaning of a new word by simply lifting a finger and pressing on that word.

You can also subscribe to magazines and newspapers or purchase books from the vast libraries of Kindle stores. There are some free e-books available on the Internet as well. You can download them and copy them into the "documents" folder of your Kindle and read them at a later time. Or you can email the book to your Kindle account and it will appear in your Kindle. Now that we are in a resource-rich era, learning becomes much easier with so many resources.

Take your Kindle with you wherever you are. You can read in the metro, on a train, on a plane, in a coffee shop, during your lunch break, or even while waiting in line. Read a few paragraphs whenever you can. Look up every new word you encounter. New words are your new friends. Pretty soon, you will accumulate a decent vocabulary and enhance your comprehension of the language.

I strongly recommend reading non-fiction books, magazines, and news articles for starters. If you are particularly interested in a certain type of book, for example, detective stories, thrillers, crime novels, romance novels, mysteries, fantasies, or even erotic stories, then you can include some fiction books on your reading list. My recommendation is not cut-and-dried. You can fine-tune your selection of reading materials based on your own interests. If you find a book engaging, you are more likely to read it enthusiastically cover to cover. Interest is the best teacher.

A client of mine is dyslexic. Fortunately, he takes a special interest in thrillers, so he reads a great number of thrillers to improve his reading skills. He now runs a company of his own. Many shortcomings can be overcome by conscious and enthusiastic efforts. You can train your mind to read and concentrate better. What's your favorite genre of books? What ignites your passion? Use your passion to your advantage.

Reading, writing, and speaking are mutually reinforcing. When you read, note down some sentences that you especially like. Use small chunks of spare time to review those sentences a few times to reinforce memorization. Read them out loud; learn them by heart if possible. In so doing, you are forced to pay close attention to how sentences are put together. Try to use those sentences in your writing and speaking wherever appropriate. Gradually, you will be able to engage in conversations in a more sophisticated manner because you have built a small database of sentences that you can draw from.

Chapter Eight – Writing

If you want to become a good writer, either in your mother tongue or in a foreign language, the first prerequisite is to be a voracious reader and avidly engage your text. You can't learn the craft of writing without investing a tremendous amount of time reading extensively first.

When writing in a foreign language, please do not write in your mother tongue first and then translate what you have written into the foreign language. It's not going to work well, not to mention it's more time-consuming than writing directly in the foreign language. Each language has its unique sentence structures, expressions, and grammar rules, which may not translate well into another language. If you are kidnapped by your own mother tongue, writing and thinking in your mother tongue first, chances are what you write may not make sense when translated into a foreign language. My advice is to wipe the writing board clean and start thinking and writing in the foreign language. Use what you know about the foreign language to write what you can. Forget about what you cannot write at the moment. If you are able to write correctly in a foreign language, even if only in simple sentences, it'll still better than translating from your mother tongue and writing awkwardly.

Do not mind starting small. No one can write The Odyssey overnight. You can start by chatting in the foreign language, writing emails, or posting on Twitter and forums. The more you write, the more comfortable you will get with writing in a foreign language.

While reading, pay special attention to diction, sentence structures, collocations, verb tenses, and how sentences are put together.

If you are an English learner, you must know that there's a multitude of ways to express the idea of "very."

For example:
She's very beautiful. - She's strikingly beautiful.
She's a very good player. - She plays exceptionally well.
I'm very impressed. - I am immensely impressed.
You're very kind. - You're incredibly kind.

Pay attention to how people talk and write and you will be able to pick up different ways of expressing the same idea. Attention to detail is what sets you apart from mediocre learners. Thirty students sit in the same classroom and listen to the same teacher, and come examinations there will be thirty different testing results. You have to be an active reader and listener to absorb information most effectively and stand out amongst the crowd.

I follow a few published writers on Twitter. I've noticed that some writers spend most of their time either reading or writing or traveling for new experiences and ideas. It takes a lot of effort to hone your writing skills.

Here's a simple exercise you can do to learn to write in a foreign language. When you read, if you see some sentences you like, rewrite them by replacing the subject while leaving the structure and most of the wording intact.

Let me give you an example to clarify:

Here's a paragraph from the book On Writing Well by William Zinsser:

"Writing is hard work. A clear sentence is no accident. Very few sentences come out right the first time or even the third time. Remember in moments of despair; if you find writing is hard, it's because it's hard."

"Learning a foreign language is hard work. Fluency is no accident. Remember in moments of despair; if you find that learning languages is hard, it's because it's hard."

By changing the subject, you can learn to describe more things in a foreign language. And it's an easy exercise to do. You will be less likely to make grammatical errors by building on existing sentences. If you keep doing this exercise, you will gradually be able to talk and write about more in a foreign language.

Chapter Nine – Dictionaries

We look up new words in a dictionary. A dictionary records almost all of the words of a language. Of course, there are always some newly coined phrases that dictionary updates cannot keep up with. If a dictionary records almost all of the words of a language, is it necessary to memorize the whole dictionary to achieve fluency? Not necessarily.

I have heard about people who have memorized a complete dictionary. I have never done that, and I don't think it is necessary or efficient. It's simply too time-consuming to memorize a bulky dictionary. As it is, many words in the dictionary are not commonly used. Unless you have too much time to kill, I don't recommend memorizing a full-length dictionary from A to Z. However, I do recommend picking up a couple of dictionaries on phrasal verbs, idioms, and conversations. Such dictionaries normally have fewer pages and offer you an opportunity to intensely study some commonly used phrasal verbs and idioms, which are an integral part of any language. Without a decent knowledge of phrasal verbs, idioms, slang, proverbs, and sayings, it's difficult to speak and write like a native speaker.

Prestigious dictionary publishers, such as Longman, Oxford, Cambridge, and Collins, have dictionaries on phrasal verbs and idioms in many languages. Just pick up a few such dictionaries and use them as textbooks to study.

Speaking of dictionaries, avoid pocket dictionaries that do not come with sample sentences. Always pick a dictionary that offers both word definition and sample sentences so that you can learn how to use a new word in context. Knowing the definition is not enough. It's more important to be able to make sentences on your own using the new words. Or at least, you can memorize some sample sentences from the dictionary so that you can use them under appropriate circumstances.

I highly recommend using a monolingual dictionary once you have built up a decent vocabulary, say about 2,000 to 3,000 words. Why use a monolingual dictionary? Meaning is always lost in translation. Only by checking the original definition can you grasp the precise meaning of a word. Using a monolingual dictionary can create a full and immersive environment for you, forcing you to read and think in the language. You will also be able to write better in the language as a result.

Don't be intimidated by a monolingual dictionary. Some dictionary publishers have done a good job of explaining words with a simple vocabulary. For example, the Longman Dictionary of Contemporary English uses a vocabulary of about 2,000 words to write definitions for words. As a result, the definitions are clear and easy to understand. Longman also offers dictionaries in many other languages. You can start by using a bilingual dictionary; once you reach the intermediate level, try using a monolingual dictionary. Just give it a shot. It has many long-term benefits.

Chapter Ten – Learn with Childlike Wonder, but Learn like an Adult

Some people say that it becomes far harder to learn a new language after puberty, but the fact is that babies and adults learn differently. It is possible for an adult to learn a new language. Many people have successfully done it, myself included.

I have noticed adults are more likely to speak with an accent, while young children who live abroad or in a bilingual family are more likely to speak like a native speaker. In my view, it's ok to have a little accent, and some may even find it interesting or charming. If you use both audio and scripts to work on your pronunciation and you do a lot of shadowing after the audios, you will be able to minimize your accent.

A language is an important tool for communication. Your top priority should be effective communication in a foreign language. The biggest failure with language learning is not being able to get your message across in the foreign language; it's not having a little accent. Don't write yourself off because of a little accent. English is the most widely used international language for trade and international conferences. People from around the world speak English with varied accents, yet they still manage to understand each other in international interactions.

It is tremendously helpful for an adult to learn with childlike wonder and be curious. When my two-year-old niece started speaking, she would ask, "What's this?" a thousand times per day. I was impressed by her enormous zest and curiosity about her surroundings. If we as adults could learn with that kind of childlike wonder, it would really work wonders. Don't be a jaded adult. Be curious like a child, and take a keen interest in the language you are learning. You're not just learning a new language, you are learning about a culture, a history, a people, an entire country.

Children usually don't worry about making mistakes, and they do not fully understand embarrassment. They just use their limited vocabulary to communicate what they are thinking, and we find it cute even when their speech is not clear or correct. We should learn from children and not worry about being judged or ridiculed. We can definitely benefit from having a childlike attitude.

As adults, we also have our own strengths and merits. Adults have stronger analytical and cognitive abilities and a longer attention span. Young children do not have the attention span to learn 100 new words per day, while adults can exercise self-discipline to make the time to learn. In this respect, adults can learn much faster than young children and be more persistent in their pursuits. As adults, we can set ambitious goals for ourselves and set out to achieve those goals with conscious efforts.

Never label yourself as "too old" to learn a foreign language or "not talented enough". Such statements are not true and they only generate self-doubt and negativity. We're all born with the innate ability to learn and grow. A can-do attitude and single-minded efforts can make a world of difference.

In the movie The King's Speech, King George VI had to overcome his stammer to become a better public speaker. With the help of a speech therapist, he practiced for about one hour per day. With coaching and practice, he finally managed to overcome his stammer and delivered an inspiring wartime speech on the radio. As I see it, the king's stammer mostly derived from some childhood trauma. His speech impediment was partly the result of self-doubt.

I believe that we're all equipped with the ability to learn languages and speak well, we just have to remove any destructive self-doubt and throw our whole being into the learning of a new language, fully convinced that we will get there one day as long as we keep trying. It's never too late to learn a new language.

I hope the methods I shared in this book help you go further in your language-learning journey. It's never too late to start this rewarding journey, which will hopefully change your mind and your life for the better if you stick with it.

I wish you every success on your journey to conquer a new language. Make sure you learn useful sentences every single day and start using them from day one, and you will have increasingly fulfilling days ahead.

The best time to begin is now. Get started now and don't you ever give up!

Printed in Great Britain
by Amazon

83662985R00037